A gift for

Theresa

from

Bea

At the HEART

of FRIENDSHIP

It's
wonderful
to have someone
whom you grow to love
for being such a great person
and such a good friend.

A wonderful friend is a beautiful blend of caring and sharing and love

At

the very

heart of friendship

there is love.

A
good friendship is
constantly changing and growing.
Depend on its beauty to delight you
and its strength to sustain you
through every season
of your life.

There
are moments
when a special friend
makes a difference
that no one
else can
make.

*A friend
is one who creates
a circle of belonging, a sacred
space in which all is safe, all is calm,
all is good.*

*One
of the secrets
of life is keeping your
friends within hugging distance.*

My
Friend

*There
are not many things
in life as beautiful as true friendship,
and there are not many things more
uncommon.*

Sharing
laughter, sharing tears,
sharing triumphs, sharing fears,
growing closer through the years…
true friendship is
forever.

A
real friend
listens with her heart
and never stops believing in you
even if you give up on
yourself.

Friendship

IS A RAINBOW

between two

hearts.

A friend

is that special

someone with whom

you always feel

at ease.

May Friends

Be True

One

of the most

beautiful qualities

of true friendship is to understand

and be understood.

Friendship is a sheltering tree.

Time endears and cannot fade the memories that love has made

Once

in a while

you will find a friend

who will be

a friend

forever.

*A true
friendship is
as wise as it is tender.*

Friendship

WEAVES BEAUTIFUL

patterns

*A friend
can make anything
better simply
by being
there.*

The very best "remember whens" are made by very special friends

I like
to think that we are
sent special friends to share our lives,
very special friends
we can be ourselves with,
talk with, laugh with, hope with...
special friends
like you.

❧

When

the news is all bad

and the sky is all gray

and the chocolate is all gone,

it's good to remember

I've got a friend

like you.

❧

Nothing on earth is more comforting than a true friendship

*A friend
understands the
unspoken thoughts in
your heart.*

*A friend
is someone who
sees you as you wish you were
and likes you as you
really are.*

*People
don't talk
much about the love
friends have for one another.*

*We talk
about liking friends,
but some friends add so much
to our lives that "like"
just isn't strong
enough.*

What a

BEAUTIFUL DIFFERENCE

your friendship has made.